THE WHITE SILHOUETTE

James Harpur has had five poetry collections published by Anvil Press and is poetry editor of the *Temenos Academy Review* and a member of Aosdána, the Irish academy of the arts. His *Angels and Harvesters* (2012) was a PBS Recommendation and shortlisted for the 2013 *Irish Times* Poetry Now Award; and *The Dark Age* (2007) won the Michael Hartnett Poetry Award. Other prizes and awards include the UK National Poetry Competition, the Vincent Buckley Poetry Prize, an Eric Gregory Award, and a Patrick and Katherine Kavanagh Fellowship. His other books include *Fortune's Prisoner*, a translation of the poems of Boethius; and *The Gospel of Joseph of Arimathea*. He lives in West Cork.

Also by James Harpur

Angels and Harvesters
2012

The Dark Age
2007

*Fortune's Prisoner: The Poems
of Boethius's Consolation of Philosophy*
2007

Oracle Bones
2001

The Monk's Dream
1996

A Vision of Comets
1993

The White Silhouette

James Harpur

CARCANET

First published in Great Britain in 2018
by
Carcanet Press Limited
Alliance House, 30 Cross Street
Manchester M2 7AQ

Printed by SRP Ltd.
A CIP catalogue record for this book is available from
the British Library, ISBN 9781784105822.

The publisher acknowledges financial assistance
from Arts Council England.

Contents

III. LEAVES

1

The White Silhouette

The Journey East

Winter 2010

The car revving up, the three of us
wiping mist away to find a whiter world.

Black ice to Clonakilty –
cortège of cars behind a spectral hearse.

Strings of lights in Bandon, sapphire-cold,
and the stars are moving through the river.

On Cork's Victorian viaduct, a train made of snow.
We steam below the River Lee.

Cork city crusts behind us;
three swans on Slatty Water; feathery ice.

The sun's last x-ray radiates the trees.
Lights turn red in Castlemartyr.

Diesel-slush road. Across the Blackwater
Waterford has drifted white.

Inching mile by mile – through Iceland? Greenland?
Wexford, another country.

Dungarvan's glittery square:
each shop an advent calendar window.

Beyond the Suir bridge the dark returns…
but angels are alighting on New Ross.

Rosslare night; chalet on a ghostly estate.
Sound of wind in chimney.

Dawn ferry, sudden vibrations –
propellers churn the sea to snow.

The swell-swing up and down and up –
O let the voyage finish now, and grant us solid earth.

From Pembroke Wales unfolds in white;
a postbox in a wall, red as a berry.

Below the Severn bridge –
water turned to bone!

The Somerset Levels, crisp and even;
the motorway accelerates the dark.

The night re-icing the Yeovil road –
not now, not now we're nearly there.

Cattistock lumped with snow;
wood incense, curtains edged with gold.

A house on Duck Street:
an outdoor light – a star that's stopped overhead.

The Perseids

August 2017

On the plateau of Bosmenditte
we watched the sky deepen
and the last Pyrenean peaks
creeping from the bronze age,
the six of us on the grass,
two lots of parents, two daughters,
assembling chairs and a table,
foraging for rotted twists of oak
to make a fire, a token of the dying sun.
We broke bread on top of the world,
poured red wine into mugs,
and alternated between
the pitter-patter of conversation
and listening to the rhythm
of clonking bells: a group of cows
had gathered by the slope's edge,
watching us with moon eyes,
their bodies cream-white.
And from a nearby tor
a dozen sheep ambled down,
approached the cows and stopped
like stationary clouds, glowing
in the still-darkening sky, our fire
the sole flickering of movement.
Until a movement on the road
between bushes – a horse galloping,
then five more, dark brown and tan,
their manes flowing like mantillas –
they halted opposite the cows
and sheep, and joined the vigil.

We lay on rugs on spongy moss
huddled for warmth, heads on stomachs,
our prayers and wishes at the ready.
And nothing came.
The animals entered dark outlines
and constellations marked the bones
of giant mythic beasts and beings,
Cassiopeia and Ursa Major,
Pegasus, Cygnus the Swan.
And still we waited, with nerves
and hearts as much as eyes,
as if we were waiting for new lives
to open up miraculously
or some spark to jolt us
into different ways of thinking.
And as we wondered, 'Will they ever come?'
three of us shouted, the others
exclaiming 'Where? Where?' –
we pointed to the interstellar spaces
and there, a streak of light, a cry of wonder,
then a rush of thicker light, its wake
fizzing like a rocket's tail,
a smaller star unzipping a patch of dark.
And on they came, popping up,
as slight as blinks
or like torches of white fire
drawn across the immensity of space –
as if a veil had fallen
and we were watching
the stirrings of the universal mind,
each cell and synapse and signal
in the firmament of its being.
Up our wishes flew, and prayers, too,
our backs moulded in the mountain top
our eyes filling with endlessness.

And in the freckled darkness
the stars looked down on us
and on the gathering of silent animals,
as if they'd willed us there, the ones
they had been waiting for,
ensouling the universe
with our thoughts for sick and absent friends
and wishes for uncertain futures –
the stars saw the meaning of life –
if only for the time it took
to see and lose a prayer
in our evaporating trails of love.

GRAVEN IMAGES

*'Simultaneously the shape of the Maiden of God changes,
as, I believe, it receives her living visitation and signifies
the invisible in the visible.'*

Michael Psellos (*c.* 1017–1078) on the unveiling of
the icon of the Virgin Mary at Blachernae

*'A Minister being then on the top of the Citie ladder, neer
60 steps high, with a whole pike in his hand ratling down
proud Beckets glassy bones ...*

*And now to end (with very good Cathedrall news from
Canterburie) ... light comes in there through the windows,
where the painted Images stood and kept it out.'*

Puritan divine, Richard Culmer, 1644

I

Bishop's Head

Late fifteenth century, Winchester Cathedral

Behind
your eyes
I can see
gold glint,
mandorla flames
of candles,
splinters
of stained glass;
can smell
the incense
your nose
relished
before
they smashed it
and left your head
to roll
in the aisle,
a gargoyle
against
the goblins
of their senses.

II

Cross

Vandalised finial cross, Rievaulx Abbey

ampu-
tated
cross
a cross
remains: phantom
limbs
remem-
bered
pain

III

Ave Maria

Annunciation frieze, Fountains Abbey

Someone
chiselled off
the features
of your face
as delicately
as a sculptor
wanting to
explore
the process
of creation,
to trace
the source
of truth or beauty
below the detail
to base stone,
Urgrund,
and finding
in the oval
of nothingness,
a certain peace
and stillness
like an astronomer
gazing at
the moon
and resting on
the shadow
of Mare
Tranquillitatis.

IV

Vision

Semi-blinded God the Father, Winchester Cathedral

O Lord
did you pluck
your own eye out?
What was your offence?

That you finally saw
the image of yourself in men,
Sons of Adam,
smiting in your name?

V

Alchemy

Madonna and Child, Winchester Cathedral

Pursuing you
for centuries
King Herod's men
at last
caught up with you
in Winchester,
and left you
a single arm
to clutch the infant
they beheaded;
then stood
and watched
the space
the halo filled –
dance again
with motes
of dust
your love
kept turning
into gold.

VI

The Raid

Decapitated Christ enthroned in majesty, Rievaulx Abbey

Toes peep out
beneath the robe:
the coast is clear.

VII

Mater

Tudor retable fragment, Whittlesford Church, Cambs

O Lady
of Whittlesford,
what do your eyes
refine beneath
those lids of alabaster?
Sleep or grief?
Or the consolation
of feeling
on your breast
that tiny little hand,
vestige
of your baby
now forever suckled
to its heart's content
on the breast
of Mother Memory?

VIII

Broken

Small wooden crucifix figure, Fiddleford Manor, Dorset

Dear Christ
chesspiece
king
arms snapped
from thorax
stick legs
head sunk
too weak
to whisper
Eli, Eli.
But still
I hear you cry
as one sees
the light
of a star
that died
two thousand
years ago.

IX

Wounds

Life-size dead Christ, Chapel of the Mercers' Company, Cheapside;
discovered in a 1954 post-war clearance

Nothing
more dead –
this corpse
on rock
seaweed hair
shell eyes
mouth-crack
dark as a tomb
from which
a body
has been taken;
hands, feet,
removed. But
the midriff gash
slit of gore
as unerasable
as the whistle
of bombs
falling;
or echo
of mallets
banging;
or scream
of nails
piercing.

X

Glass

Collected from Rievaulx and Furness abbeys

Fragments
spilled across
a light box
like loose change:
dark shapes –
trapezoid
arrowhead
knapped flint;
inklings
of colours,
bottle green
salmon pink
lapis lazuli;
a hint of a face.
How little
the imagination
needs
to see
the invisible:
a shepherd
in a field
of Galilee;
a ladder
of angels
ascending
and descending.

Headless Angels

In St Nicholas's Church, Galway city

When they saw you – Cromwell's troopers
stabling their horses in nave and choir –
did they remember the angels at Mamre
receiving a blessèd welcome in the desert?

Or Daniel's angel in his linen clothes,
his loins girded with gold of Uphaz?
Or the angel who rolled back the stone,
face like lightning, raiment white as snow?

And seeing your fiery wings made material,
did they rage against the dull, heavy world?
Or were they blinding any witness to their crime –
concealing in the priest holes of their minds

a grain
of imagination?

The Face

Icon of Christ the Redeemer, Andrei Rublev, Tretyakov Gallery

I turned a corner and saw your eyes
as if *you* had turned a corner
in the moonlight of a deserted city
and seen me looking in surprise
at the faded colours
of your disembodied, floating face.
I wanted to touch it
like the woman daring to touch the edge
of your robe to heal herself.

I want to touch that moment again
before the wood reclaims you
forever, withdraws you into its grain,
your features too unearthly,
too full of light for this world,
assaulted by the stares of believers
and unbelievers, erasing you
second by second, day by day,
with too much hope, or idle curiosity.

Trinity

Icon of the Trinity, Andrei Rublev, Tretyakov Gallery

We had gone to Moscow on a journey
from the suburbs of Dublin
and scattered townlands of West Cork,
flying eastward into darkness,
a night of prehistoric stars,
millennia of Christianity evolved
in our names: Joseph, John and James.
And then we came, at last, to stand
in timelessness before our heritage,
forgetful of belief and unbelief.
We had the icon to ourselves,
like three angels, invisible, or making
the crowds in the gallery invisible;
conforming to a gentle communion,
sharing thoughts, bits of knowledge,
subsiding to colour, inherent gold,
the inner circularity of the tableau,
we felt our selves dissolving...
three strangers in the desert of Mamre,
sharing the freedom of wanderers
rejoicing in the chance events
and small miracles of life –
an oak tree spreading out its shade,
a little water, morsels of bread –
and snatches of words and sounds
that stir to life the unpredictable:
the whispers of Abraham at his tent,
Sarah's mocking gasp of laughter –
the prospect of a birth,
two becoming three,
three becoming one.

The White Silhouette

For John F. Deane

'There went a whisper round the decks one morning, "We have a mysterious passenger on board." … Often I thought of that rumour after we reached Jerusalem … When I saw the man all in white by the Golden Gate carrying in all weathers his lighted lamp, I always thought, "There is a mysterious pilgrim in Jerusalem."'

Stephen Graham, from *With The Russian Pilgrims to Jerusalem* (1913)

I thought we would meet in a holy place
Like the church in the hamlet of Bishopstone
Empty on a Wiltshire summer's day
The trees full of rooks and hung in green
And the stream in the meadows a rush
Of darkling silver beneath the bridge
Where I saw my first kingfisher flash
Its needle, leaving its turquoise stitch
In my memory. And I would sit
In the church and close my eyes
And wait in vain for something to ignite,
And wonder whether this was my life
Wasting away in my mother's home.
Sometimes I'd bring Herbert's *Temple*
And read the quiet order of his poems
And picture him, as once he was glimpsed,
Hugging the floor in his church at Bemerton
Asking love to bid him welcome.
I sat with an upright praying disposition
Preoccupied in self-combing
Too callow and spiritually impatient
To notice if you had slipped in
As a tourist to inspect the choir or font
And buy a picture postcard and sign

The book with 'lovely atmosphere';
Or as a walker taking refuge from rain
Or a woman primping flowers by the altar.

Or somewhere like the island of Patmos
Out of season and the tourist flow,
The sea leeching blue from the skies.
In the cave of St John, pointillist gold
On tips of candles and highlights of icons,
You might have visited that day in September
When I was there, absorbing the coolness,
Imagining John on the Day of the Lord
Prostrate on the ground as if before a throne
And you not dressed in a 'robe and gold sash'
Nor with hair 'as white as wool or snow'
But as a pilgrim with camera and rucksack
Respectful, curious, guidebook in hand
Appreciating the grain of raw stone
Catching my eye and pausing for a second
As if I were a schoolfriend from years ago.
I never saw you, if you were there,
For I was too blinded by the new Jerusalem
Flashing out jasper, topaz, sapphire,
Descending from heaven like a huge regal crown.

Or somewhere like Holycross in Tipperary,
The abbey at the meeting of road and river,
You might have stopped to break a journey
As I often do, and seen me there in the nave
Ambling down the sloping floor
Towards the relic-splinter of the Cross
Or sitting outside on the banks of the Suir
On a bench on a swathe of tended grass
Perhaps that day when, heading north,
I paused by the car park to watch

A bride, fragile, and frozen by the door
Her bridesmaids huddled in the cold of March
Waiting and waiting to make her entrance
Into the sudden shine of turning faces
Like a swan gliding in its snowdress
From an arch of the bridge in a state of grace.
I was too mesmerised by her destiny
To see you start your car, drive off,
And raise your hand as you passed me by
On the way to Cashel, Fermoy and the south.

But there was that time I was so certain
That I had finally found you;
Sick at home, I turned to meditation
And prayer to overcome self-pity
For weeks accumulating quietude
Till that morning when seconds were emptied out
My thoughts cleansed, my self destroyed
Within an uncanny infusing light
That seemed to deepen and unfold
More layers of radiance and lay me wide open
So you could cross the threshold
Or I could cross, at any moment.
But I closed the door of my heart, afraid,
Who knows, that I might have met you,
Afraid I would pass to the other side
And never return to all that I knew;
I thought I could always re-open myself
And greet you properly, well prepared.
I never did. I feared that sudden shift
Into the zone of timelessness; too scared
I looked for you in public, for safety,
I kneeled in churches, gave the sign
Of peace in St James's Piccadilly;
I recited prayers, took bread and wine

And I concentrated so hard, but failed
To believe they were your blood and body;
I heard staccato prayers, like nails
Banged in, as if to board up windows.

Sometimes I'd sense you as a glimmer
As in that dream I once had out of the blue
When you stood at night on a Greek island shore;
Your face was hidden, but it was you;
The stars pinned in place the layers of darkness;
Then came the comets, perhaps a dozen,
Their tails fanned out with diminishing sparks;
Slowly they twisted and turned – your hands
Moving in concert, as if you were guiding them,
As if they were on strings, like Chinese kites.
The comets slowed and stopped, and changed
Into letters of Hebrew, emblazoning the night.
And I knew if I could grasp those words,
Your silent message across the stars,
I'd know my destiny on earth.
Instead I woke, as puzzled as Belshazzar.

I do not search for you any more
I don't know whom to seek, or where;
Too weary, disillusioned, I'm not sure
What I think or if I really care
That much; my last hope – that my resignation
Might be a sign of the Via Negativa,
A stage of my self-abnegation –
Prevents the thing it hopes for.

And yet

I still write to you, poem after poem,
Trying to shape the perfect pattern

Of words and the mystery of their rhythm,
An earthly music audible in heaven –
Each poem is a coloured flare
A distress signal, an outflowing
Of myself, a camouflaged prayer
dispatched towards the Cloud of Unknowing
And all I have to do is stay
Where I am, ready to be rescued
Not move, speak or think but wait
For the brightening of the Cloud
For your white silhouette to break
Free from it and come nearer, nearer,
Till I see your essence and I can ask
Where in the world you were
Throughout my days – and only then
Will I grasp why I never found you
Because you were too close to home
Because I thought I'd have to die
To see you there, right there, removing
The lineaments of your disguise –
My careworn wrinkled skin
My jaded incarnation of your eyes –
My face becoming your face
My eyes your eyes
I   you   us   I you us
Iesus.

2

Kells

for Francesca Diano, with deep gratitude and affection

'In order to paint you, O Virgin, stars rather than colours would be needed, so that you, the Gate of Light, should be depicted in luminosities. But the stars do not obey the voices of mortals. Therefore we delineate and paint you with what nature and the laws of painting can provide.'

Constantine of Rhodes, ninth century

'In the degree in which beauty is diffused by entering into matter, it is so much the weaker than that concentrated in unity.'

Plotinus

'For we are but travellers on a journey without as yet a fixed abode; we are on our way, not yet in our native land; we are in a state of longing, not yet of enjoyment.'

St Augustine, Sermon 103

Goldsmith

Book of Kells, Folio 34r Matthew 1.18 Chi Rho

'*Christi autem generatio sic erat...*'
('This is how the birth of Jesus Christ came about...')
Matthew 1.18

'*Françoise Henry termed the first and greatest of [the Kells' artists] "goldsmith",
because his use of yellow and silvery blue ... were suggestive of metalwork.*'
Bernard Meehan, *The Book of Kells*

Evening was slanting the boat
from Mull towards Iona,
a journey the echo of a shout,
and I was staring at the water
as deeply as a gold panner.
Behind, Dalriada rose
in heather-lit mountains, the border
of a kingdom of shadows.
I came for traces of Columba
and found nothing but stone
in the wind-sleeted abbey,
grave slabs sliding into ruin,
the slatey boarding house
of widow hush, netless glare.
No clues on the coastal paths,
or on the rhythmic machair's
hummocky grass and furze;
or at the 'cove of the coracle'
where Columba saw, at last,
that Ireland was invisible;
or on Síthean Mor's rise
where a circle of angels appeared
as he prayed alone on his knees

and they caressed the air
with beating wings, an oratorio
of swans, alighting in a halo.

★

Pilgrims rarely find their end:
their shimmering shrines
hold nothing but bones, gems,
and wax saints. They try again
as if the journey were an end
in itself, rehearsal for death, say.
Or acting from the intuition
of a buried spiritual memory,
they trek to chapels, springs
or wells, mimicking the path
of all created things returning
to their uncreated source:
the Fountain
of ever-flowing light
that pours out forms, or patterns,
from which our world derives –
a round of cosmic *exitus*,
then earthly *redditus*...

   Pilgrims follow webs of paths
and bridleways and dirt tracks
or Roman roads and twisty lanes;
they chance on rivers, lakes,
or skirt a bog or ditch,
but their vision's always straight,
directed by a will to reach
a specific redemptive end.
Yet what happens when we dare
to be as bold as *peregrini* –
monks who cast away their oars
to let the spirit in the wind
direct them on their journey?

Just as the Magi trusted a star
or Columba exiled on the sea
was led by wind and wave to where
he found his Home, a landfall
where home was now invisible.

*

An attic in a Scottish castle,
Hawthornden, a world away;
I have paper, a postcard –
in which I struggle to decipher
Christi generatio –
and an urge to write. I'm blank,
as if sitting an examination
with questions in white ink.
Through the steepling window
I watch a torrent foaming west,
daffodils tipped with snow,
skeletal scripts of trees.
April is stiff in sap and cell.
I'm primed for the 'poetic trance'
but the urgings of my will
have failed again to let silence
descend and glimmer, like the sunrise
before it's sprung the earth
from night, and birds are poised
to break the suspense
and loosen lines of praise
to *auctorem regni caelestis*.
The paper on my desk
remains a sheet of ice.
I breathe deep; the rhythm
withdraws me layer by layer
like the whispering repetition
of the Jesus Prayer,
a steady sea-hush of breath…

the window pane's a frame
of potent tonelessness –
I gaze and let Iona come:
a blur, a silhouetted figure,
a monk, cell, scribal lectern.
He sharpens a feather,
mutters to the muffled ocean:

'Direct my hand, O Lord, my choice of pigment.
And tell me: am I to follow human likeness,
or any likeness of the world?
My fingertips are grey, my nose frozen,
my will weakened by Hesychios the Priest
who says only a heart devoid of images
can incubate your presence.
My vellum has the sacred gleam
of absence; no lines, words. Just light.
How can I enhance *Nothingness*?
And yet what lies there, waiting to leap
like porpoises from the sea, free to suck
the air and revel in weightlessness?
Or rise like tendrils into sunshine,
virile and untouched by purpose?
To make your image we must gaze on you;
to gaze on you we must become like you –
each day we fast, pray, discipline our bodies
as if they were dung-tailed beasts –
yet we feast on colours, and make vellum
as smooth as pure Byzantine silk –
we cherish the senses we must annihilate.
Lord, I must paint you. But how?
In flesh and blood, a saggy thing,
as followers of Arius would do?
Or a spirit-flash – will-o'-the-wisp –
a wraith of the monophysites?'

I watch him watch the vellum
inflict its infinite paralysis.
I think: 'Christ' is not a 'person'
but *energeia*, *lux fluens*,
the ceaseless flow of light that moves
il sole e l'altre stelle
and seeds the sort of love
that blossoms when self has lost itself.
I think: Christ cannot be painted,
but only his effect on nature –
creation that's been *Christed*.
I want to tell the monk: Surrender!
Then what's beyond the cave
of your tiny sheltered self
will swarm in – like bees to clover –
and spin like Ezekiel's wheels –
your work will be an ark – for lions,
eagles, snakes, and angels,
who move invisible among us –
and lines of Christlight threading us all
together at the level of the soul.
I say nothing. His hand is still,

*

The days trickle to a thaw,
buds are stickier on the trees,
daffodils unpeel into yellow
along the sides of the ravine.
I dream, daydream, and see Iona
on my page, the monk frozen.
One time I watch him after Vespers
on White Strand, the ocean
expunging a day of failure.
We watch the night re-seal the sky
with darkness, and Orion emerge
above Dalriada, as if a scribe

were pricking out the cosmic vellum –
its belt of stars as still and glittery
as the Kings kneeling in the stable.
Christi autem generatio.
   He leaves the sea to its ceaseless amens,
returning to the burden
of the abbey, and sleep's revenge.
His cell is cold as a cavern.
He starts to pray and confess
and I hear him in the darkness.

'Lord, I miss the valley of the Humber,
its bitter Anglian light.
Iona is adrift at sea, and I drift
from accidie to melancholia.
Each day reveals the tatters
of your creation; driftwood, seaweed,
fungus, mold, satanic mist,
the ache of flesh, a bent neck.
If creation were merely craft
I'd be content to take my knife,
prick holes, draw lines, circles.
But every dot begins a shape
I fear will mock you.
I seek purity in crushed pigment
to cleanse my brain of thought.
Yet I dread my empty mind
will mirror the emptiness of death.
How do I paint you Lord?
What eyes, nose, mouth?'

I hear his words, and hear Plotinus
discouraging a portrait painter:
'It's bad enough to bear these features
conferred on me at birth.

Why would I want to leave an image
of my image to posterity?'
I focus on the monk's face
and wonder what to say to him...
Do not depict the likeness of things
but the Ideas from which they arise –
not a rose, but *Rose,* in which
a rose will be the essence
of all roses; don't glorify the beautiful
alone, or just the saintly and sacred:
include the verminous, marginal,
crooked; and when you meditate
allow your thoughts to wilt and die –
then afterwards, in silence, you may discern
the divine in everything you see:
your brush will be a lantern
illuminating our path
towards the Imagination, its beam
of light, like a flow of *energeia,*
destroying the veil between seer and seen.

And he, as if musing to himself:
'Can vellum be a home for Christ?
Can he be circumscribed by lines –
who's like the wind, or ocean shifting
from formlessness to formlessness?'

I think: *paint formlessness* – paint it
through form: Christ was spirit *and* flesh,
and painting incarnates the spirit.
Don't think! Let go – and your brush
will catch the spirit and sail across
the mysterium of your page
and see riches in its depths;
have faith; the image will emerge.

He looks as if he wants to leap
into the blank vellum, while I
am poised to put pen to paper –
together, perhaps, we see Chi
running for joy through space –
as if bearing the tremendous news
that spring has burst at last –
its diamond core retaining stillness,
a keyhole to a world beyond;
and now it's leaving Rho behind
kicking away from moons and suns –
it differentiates, and becomes.

Scribe B

Book of Kells, Folio 183r, Mark 15.24–25

'Et crucifigentes eum diviserunt vestimenta ...
erat autem hora tercia et crucifixerunt eum.'
('And when they had crucified him, they parted his garments ...
And it was the third hour, and they crucified him.')
Mark: 15:24–25

'On folio 183r [Scribe B] intruded the words Et crucifigents eum
divise [runt] *in a space near the foot of the page, duplicating the line*
from ... the facing page.'
Bernard Meehan, *The Book of Kells*

'Writing blurs your eyes, give you a stoop, stabs your ribs and stomach, makes
your kidneys throb and afflicts your whole body.'
Florentius, tenth-century Iberian scribe

In Monaco it's always noon.
Apartment blocks surge seaward
in a permanent standing ovation;
among palm trees, boulevards,
the bobbing whitewash of yachts,
beaches with zen-raked pebbles,
no one grows old, just more sedate.
To this Grimaldi citadel
I came like Brendan landing on
the Island of Eternal Youth,
unsure if it were hell or heaven.
In the old town I took refuge
in chiaroscuro alleyways
immaculately roofed in blue
by narrow streams of sky.
And there the Irish Library

became a home – *nostalgie*
of marble stairs, Edwardian lift,
the Irish flag on the balcony
draping colour over the street;
a copy of *Kells*, its Latin words
processing syrup-slow,
their tops as trim as hedges,
redolent of the idea
that every letter must have beauty:
the m's aqueduct of arches
luxurious curves of c's
the l's delicate eyelashes.
Each word bore its lineage,
a copied copy of a copy
retreating to the not-word world,
the silence after *sabachthani*.

⋆

Home finally finds you
when the self, searching
endlessly for a country,
city or neighbourhood,
or fellowship of seekers,
convinced that somewhere
on this earth awaits it,
surrenders
from exhaustion or despair;
or a Damascus moment
when it's engulfed with light,
or 'spirit', from beyond,
and afterwards, euphoric,
it feels un-strange everywhere,
just as Plotinus said:
'Our home is where we were
before we were born;
we cannot return by foot,

for our feet only carry us
to places in this world.
Shut your eyes and wake
to a different way of seeing.'

   At this moment of seeing
we lose our scouring eyes
and enter the Imagination;
or have a sudden anamnesis,
just as Rilke, in Toledo
for the first time, knew
he'd been there once before
in a painting by El Greco:
Toledo after a thunderstorm,
light ploughing the earth
and swirling across
the violent green of hills.
He stepped out from the painting
onto the Tagus bridge,
and saw the evening anointed
by a shooting star.

   The I creates its exile
from home, becomes a stranger
to everyone and itself.
It feels the need to die,
to shed itself of self;
but wants to seed itself,
to brand itself on the world,
a drive to self-apotheosis
that widens the separation
from the divine
it cannot bear to lose.

   ★

In blazing Monaco I pale
beneath the electric bulb,
cross-eyed with *Kells,*

with insular majuscule,
nests of snakey lines
that lead the eye to nowhere –
the trails of faceless scribes
unknown except in whispers
scrawled in vellum margins
across Europe, lonely voices
beside the marching legions
of Vulgate uncials:

'The ink's poor quality,
the parchment's running out;
the day is getting darker.'

'Ah, blackbird, you're happy
with your home in the hedge.
O hermit, your lullaby
is so much softer than a bell.'

'Tonight a bitter wind
curls the tops of waves.
No need to fear the Northmen
coursing on the sea.'

I read a page by Scribe B:
Erat autem hora tercia.
Beneath the sculpted words I see
et crucifigentes eum divise
like a scrawl of red graffito
below the frieze of a temple,
or appearing magically
like the Writing on the Wall.
Outside, the sun is in retreat.
The windows across the lane
await the applying of gold leaf.

I close my eyes to open them:

Blur of trees, yews,
delapidated walls.
I'm back in Kells,
five summers before,
hunting for a house,
another quest
in search of home,
lured by the idea
of ruined choirs,
rooks in traceries
of broken light,
a great scriptorium.
But there I saw
a Protestant church,
huge stone cuckoo
its wings enfolding
a capless tower –
factory chimney
releasing in the air
invisible smoke
of silence;
and there, too,
like a pillar of salt
a rain-eroded cross
that tried to flee
the Reformation
but looked back;
and an oratory
steep as an alpine hut,
as void of prayer.
    I re-imagine
the broken abbey:
the crosses, chapel,

cells, become intact.
Like a sundial
the tower casts
a shadow across
the cropped grass.
A bell rings.
I follow a path
to the scriptorium.
The door is open.
Waft of damp;
deep-set window,
soft light, lectern.
Scribe B sitting,
staring at vellum,
quill poised,
a heron by a stream.
I look over his shoulder.
He stabs the margin.
⋆
That summer
the swallows never came.
It was as if they knew.

Three ships approaching;
north wind
writhing in their sails.

Bell: an idiot's tongue
blabbing *run, run*.

They strode through waves
that rose resistingly,
then bowed in obeisance.

Hens, flightless;

foxes taking their time.

On the white sands of White Strand
a row of bodies, whitening.

How easily a blade
cuts flesh, like vellum!

We buried the dead;
the dead burying the dead.

The sun put on a veil;
hawthorns stooped to pray
in the venting of the wind.

Live life as if death
were just a tide away.
Avoid the seaward glance
and pray for storms,
a clear horizon.

*

Exiled from exile
rowing south and west,
stout sail – seven porpoises
to point the way!

Straining for the motherland
as if necks could stretch us closer.

Landfall.
Circle of prayers
arms horizontal
numb as oars.

Each day we head towards

the setting sun; each day
we're never nearer.

Broken sandal.
God knows
where we are going.

Above treetops –
a round tower.
Crows drunk on laughter.

    Miracle.
 Home. Kells. Home.
    Miracle.

★

A life resurrected.
Or buried alive?

No starfish, waves,
but herbal light
greening our souls.

Windrush of oaks –
sea-surge on sand –
If I forget thee, Iona!

Lord, help me heal myself
by the art of letters –
circles plump as apples,
verticals with spear tips,
crossbars fine as hairs.

The wind is deep tonight
et crucifigentes eum
my sleep is hollow

et crucifigentes eum
et crucifigentes eum

I dreamed Columba spoke:
'You are God's instrument.
Your thumb and fingers
have little use without an open heart:
your quill is Aaron's rod
creating blossoms and ripe almonds.
Holy words turn ink
into a sacrament, like wine.'
*

Words copied in rage, blotch.
Words written in silence
can still be full of noise.

What use a holy book
that can't deter the teeth of mice,
or bite of swords?

My face says: *Ecce, nemo!*
My heart burns for praise.

If God wants witnesses
for his creation, *why* such a sin
to want the same for mine?

Fleck of froth
on waves of scribal duties.

Another endless
day of endless
rows of endless
words.

Cassiodorus says: writing inflicts
a wound on Satan.
Who is wounding me?

The open door –
stars of daisies,
a dandelion sun;
only the air between us.

How strange
that ink-strokes
when left unguided
find a way to draw
wild flowers
between the lines?

Outside: wagtails, bees,
whitethorn, hazel.
Inside: nibs, liquid soot.
*
Any moment
a bell shout scream
could be the end
running at us.

A tremble in my hand;
my heart a butterfly
that never flies away...

A stripe of sun bestows
an aura on the lines:
the peace of Ireland fills the room.

Third hour of the day.
the sky crow-dark.

I am a scribe.
You are nothing.
I am myself.
You are nothing.
You are God.
I am Nothing.

'Impress your self on vellum.
The page is your afterlife.'
Get thee behind me.

Do I fear death?
Or just extinction?

My final testimony:
I took the knife, pricked
the centre of my palm,
mixed droplets with red lead,
dipped my nib in it and poured
rage, grief, immortality,
into every single letter.

et crucifigentes eum divise

Gerald of Wales

Book of Kells, Folio 202v, Temptation of Christ

'Si filius dei es, mitte te hinc deorsum'
('If you are the Son of God, throw yourself down from here.')
Luke 4:9

'Among all the miracles of Kildare, nothing seems to me more
miraculous than that wonderful book which they say was written at the
dictation of an angel during the lifetime of the Virgin.'
Gerald of Wales, 1185

The British Library silence,
Trappist looks and gestures;
roof windows filter sunlight
on desks, books, researchers,
the quiet order of shelves;
the readers on a pilgrimage
to fill the absence in their lives
with a word, line or page.
And every head is crowned
by an aura of desk-lamp gold,
turning the chamber into how
I picture the mind of God,
or De Chardin's 'noosphere',
in which pure consciousness
from those who have evolved
over aeons, streams forth
as ribbons of light converging
in the knot of the omega point.
    The library in the afternoon;
researchers lingering at lunch
in Bloomsbury or St Pancras,
where the first leaves of autumn

are dropping in the squares
and patterning the pavements.
I turn a page of *Kells*:
Jesus stands on the temple
below a hovering of angels
and dominates the centre –
the halo of a claret sun
behind his tumbling golden curls –
as he shelters his brethren
from enticements of the devil,
who's soot-dipped, scrawny-small,
a fly flattened on the vellum,
repeating ad nauseam
Si filius dei es, mitte te hinc deorsum

I can appreciate the image:
the angels drifting high, so light,
the bluey-green of the temple,
and Satan's beetle-blackness. Yet
it leaves me cold. My spirit
is drilled with *curiositas*
and not the warmth of worship.
Does sacred art suffuse us
with a sense of the Beyond?
Or does it make a barrier?
And if it makes us feel connected
to the divine and one another
can copies of it do the same?
Do eyes, ears – and souls –
seek out symmetrical forms,
harmonies, gold and jewels
as echoes of the Light?
Or should we shun our senses
and empty out our hearts
to make a space for Light to enter?

On one side: Bernard of Clairvaux,
mystic of love, crusade-monger,
who rated bodily delights as dung
and railed at artefacts of abbeys,
the faceted flash of candelabra:
'What's the point of these things?
To gain contrition, or admiration?
In cloisters, where we study
or rest our minds in simplicity,
we're assaulted by menageries
of sculpted centaurs, soldiers, apes,
hunters blowing their horns,
some creature with a serpent's tail.
and so we marvel at grotesqueries
instead of contemplating God.'

On the other side: Abbot Suger.
I see him enter St Denis alone,
pausing to read the gilded doors:
Mens hebes ad verum
per materialia surgit.
Inside his New Jerusalem
he sees that his creation's good:
light raw and pure from heaven
is rainbowed over stone and gold;
the altar erupts in amethysts.
'Sometimes in this house of God
the glint of gemstones
withdraws me from external cares,
and through material things
my dull mind rises to truth –
I seem to see myself existing
in a realm beyond this world.'
★

In slivers of harvest moons
the desk lamps darken the day
in the vast glass library roof,
as if cosmic consciousness is fading.
The room is emptying. I prepare
to summon Gerald of Wales.
My screen is liquorice black. I peer
as if looking in a crystal ball
and see a misty human form:
Gerald, sitting by a hearth,
firelit face, pale as rigor mortis.
He unpinches his mouth.

'Everything is meaningless.
All come from dust, all journey back to dust.
I left eternity in Kildare.

                    I remember
my carriage trundling into town...
the abbey lumbering towards me,
great sad beast; puddles on flagstones,
the monks a-froth with tales
of things contrary to nature –
a salmon glinting gold teeth,
a werewolf who begged a priest
to grant him absolution.
And then their story of the Gospel book.

'The night before a certain monk
was due to paint a page
he dreamt an angel proffered him
a tablet etched with silver circles
enclosing threads of gold.
Between circles, lines crossed
like swallows skimming fields;
their ends split up and curved

away, entwined again, were spun
towards the firmament
by figures of saints and animals
in gold and dragonfly viridian.
The angel asked the monk
if he could copy what he saw,
and when he shook his head
the angel bade him pray to Brigid
to ask the Lord to scrape away
impediments of earthly dross
and open up his spiritual eye.

   Next night the angel came again
with other tablets filigreed
as if with webs picked off the grass.
The monk, his vision opened
by prayer, could now absorb
each circle, arc and interlace,
each flower, animal and saint,
from the minutiae to the whole.
Next day he settled down to paint
and needed no invention:
he simply copied what he'd seen.

   Imagination is nothing but
the recollection of the holy.

'Next day I go alone to see the book.
I follow my ghostling breath inside
the chapter house towards the lectern,
as if walking on tiptoe, a wren
inside my ribcage. The book's open.
I shut my eyes and then
a whirligig of coloured noise
disjunctive shapes, an ark of chaos
and all I taste is yellow bile –
I haven't come a hundred miles to see

a god-forsaken quag
                            I force myself
to stare, and stare, with equanimity,
and I'm nothing if not disciplined:
as if looking through
                                    the surface of a pond
for something hidden
                                    in the shadow water
among reeds and stones
                                and there, *a carp*
lit up
            a scrap of sunset –
just so my eyes adjusted to the vellum:
Christ on the temple roof
his eyes softening my soul
as if he had been waiting all this time
for me to come to him
                                    and in the air
whispered words, quiet as a kiss,
and though I'd heard them
so many times before, I heard them now
as if my heart alone were listening –
You shall worship the Lord your God,
him only shall you serve –
sharp lights assailed me – flurry
of shooting stars – for a breath
I thought a vision was being granted me at last
but no, the images began to blur
as if I were too high, too giddy –
worship the Lord – it came again
and then I heard *If you are the Son of God,*
throw yourself down from here
and I stabbed the devil with my knife,
and stabbed
then gripped the book like a bridle

until my feet became good solid feet,
then solid legs and torso, solid neck
and all fell into place again.
Unable to look Christ in the face
I turned the page, kept turning,
and felt the golden lines reel in my eye
then promptly lose it –
as a blackbird lures then cheats the ear
with song, or as the grace notes of a harp
rise and dive and rise
above the sonorous melody:
Si latet, ars prodest –
concealed art is a mirror of the soul.

'Who knows how long I wandered in
the mind of God before creation?
Each page delivered me
from my self-created rutted path
towards the see of St David's –
the only prize I'd coveted
from childhood, when on the shore
I'd build churches out of sand.
To this end: a life of careful tact,
selective showings of humility
that never led me anywhere beyond
the petitioner's path to Rome –
six months there, and six back –
to kiss the ring of the pope.
And all for what?
A Welsh archdeaconate.
Within the vellum of that book
lines sprouted like destinies
I'd missed, rejected or ignored.
Faced with the patterns of life –
the template of the infinite –

my sense of being *me* eroded,
my will to advancement died.
Once chance I had to turn to Him
and end my exile in his arms.
One chance. Perhaps I should've jumped
from the temple, perhaps Christ –
not Satan – was telling me to jump,
to trust myself
to the awful weightlessness of the unknown.
What might have been endures
inside my heart, a pecking ghost
feeding on self-recrimination.

'Now by the waters of Lincoln,
my diocese of god-forsaken fen,
I weep when I remember Kildare.
The image of that book is like
an ever-fading, never-faded bruise.
My mind wanders like a Jew.
My face has now become
the death mask of my soul,
and everything is meaningless.

'Beauty is not so much a thing
as a moment, unrepeatable,
although the moment needs the thing
as a flame needs a wick
or images a page.
Or it's a streak of lightning
connecting heaven to earth
whereby in a flash we breathe
the enormity of something Other
beyond our tiny grasping selves
and fill our lungs with it,
before the dark returns again.

The soul expands with beauty –
it cannot help itself; our task in life
is to prevent it shrinking back.'

Verbum

Book of Kells, Folio 292r, John 1:1

'In principio erat Verbum...'
('In the beginning was the Word...')
John 1:1

'It is incomparably easier to love if one remains silent than if one talks.
The care of searching for words greatly obstructs the movement of the heart.'
Jean Hamon, *Traité de Pieté*, 1689

A winter's day, a summer house
perched high on a rock in a garden;
a low enclosing stone wall sprouting
ivy and ferns; on the horizon
the illumined hill of Carrigfada,
three turbines turning lackadaisically,
a sun-struck vision of Golgotha;
and, nearer, outsize Christmas trees
edging bogland, inlets of fields;
a stream runs parallel with the road
that sloughs it off and winds up hill
to the grotto of the peeling Virgin,
a graveyard, pub, church.
To the north, the Boggerah mountains;
the Atlantic ocean to the south.
This summer house is my summit,
a shrine of panoramas, terminus
of the concatenation of events
and chance or synchronistic meetings
with people, which convince me
my path could not have been otherwise.
The door is open; below, within
the brittle tangle of a furze

a wren is trilling, invisible,
as if the bush is trilling, pizzicato;
shadows creep towards the stone wall.
I look at a postcard: *In Principio*.

*

In the beginning is Shankill,
  the train glides behind back-gardens,
marginalia of sheds, bins, bicycles,
names of stations stutter-slurring
  into clarity; then off we go again,
our journey lined by banks and fencing
except for glimpses of the strand
  the long horizon
and waves erasing watermarks from sand.
From Pearse Street, the world
  accumulates again in flickerings
of Christmas in shops along the roads.
In Trinity I sense the holy relic:
  a queue of pilgrims,
the antechamber of trinkets.

I join the shuffling stop-start line
as edgy as a mourner filing past
a waxy body in an open box,
I know I'll only have a minute
or so, my eyes are two hair-triggers
I'm nearly there, nearly there,
bang –
as if I've just been shoved on stage
adjusting to the sepia audience –
I see the gospel squiggle into life
with oblongs, circles branded on
as frames to trap the golden bees
so quick they fly invisibly
but leave an afterglow in ribbons

of countless plaited flights –
a dream from someone's sleep
pressed on vellum like a transfer –
swathe of skin assaulted by
a mad tattooist – blueprint
of creation by the Demiurge,
planets spinning in his eyes
his paintbrush touching things to life –
a brain whirring inside out,
the electrics of a migraine.
I take a breath.
I feel like St John, a sad alchemist
in his lab of bubbling cylinders
who yet again has failed to find
the lapis philosophorum –
I blur my focus
and the less I stare the more I see,
letters begin to creep from foliage
like members of a species
thought to be extinct –
there's someone nudging me to move,
Let it come, let it come,
another thirty seconds, please,
and yes, it's there, pristine and freed
In
Prin-
ci-
pio erat   Verbum.

I buy a postcard. Outside
    in dimming courtyards
the wind skims my face with ice,
propels me to the gate.
    I want to walk somewhere, metabolise
the page I've seen – I let my feet dictate

rhythm and direction
   and turn from Nassau into Dawson Street
and watch the doleful face of John
emerge, then *In Principio* appears,
   its blue initials stepped and cut
like giant medieval keys;
other letters start to surface –
   an *I* becomes a harpist
plucking an elongated *C* –
everything shifts and slides –
   the book proclaims the Gospel
in words as unambiguous as light
and yet the concert of its patterns suggests
   reality as sinuous flux –
perhaps the book's a mirror of consciousness
or a map, or a maze designed
   to lure the brain towards a centreless centre
and madden it with lines of lines
until, short-circuited, it sees Truth –
   as at Emmaus, when the bread was snapped,
the stranger was revealed as Jesus.
These threads slip off to other paths –
   my feet turn left for Molesworth Street,
St Stephen's Green; I puff around the park
then spin off north and back to Trinity
   and reach O'Connell Bridge,
and stop and watch the Liffey:
The quays, car-crushed, gleam
through stalks of winter trees,
kinetic red, amber, green.
I am a once-and-only witness
of the Great Book of Dublin,
its pages divided by the river,
a shifting fiery pointillism –
mens surgit per materialia –

and nothing can be reproduced
for everything flows –
lights, movement, noise –
and everything is now and once.
*

Home can be an island or scriptorium,
a chapel or a book,
a place or spiritual condition
you enter like a déjà vu,
dissolving in its sudden stillness.
Or is home a place of transit
to a place of transit? An *epektasis*,
ascent to God, step by step,
when every stage you reach impels
your soul to persevere
towards the never-reachable,
as when we climb a hill and there,
revealed, another higher range
inspiring a further trek:
we leave, arrive, and leave again
ascending peak to peak,
an effortless continuum
ad gloriosum infinitum.
*

Dublin leaves the summerhouse.
I contemplate my postcard
of *In Principio*; nothing comes.
I doodle a face in lieu of words,
long black hair, almond eyes,
high cheekbones, like a goddess –
Athena, Isis, perhaps a Muse –
a flowing pleated dress;
crosshatching frames her shape,
hypnotic in its self-creation.
I pause, meditate on her face

and listen
until there's just my breath,
a steady sibilant pulse;
silence…
words slip from her mouth:

'You can be a witness of creation
and recreate it from the known –
the evidence of eyes or memory,
artfully shaped, polished
and interwoven with imagination.
But this won't lead to truth.
To make true images of things
you think you must become them
with an infinitely empathising self.
But if, without your interfering I,
you did become a rose, or wind,
there'd be no need to recreate it;
why would a rose describe a rose?
Fullness of being is sufficient to itself.
To that extent all art is sadness,
a sign of failed communion
with what it tries to frame or capture.
Look at the sadness of St John –
perhaps the face of the scribe himself
knowing his artifice was merely
a measurement of distance from Life,
Verbum, the divine source,
or whatever you want to call me.

'Remember this.
I do not have a name or face, or form,
and words and paint prolong the lie
that I can be depicted: I am beyond
all sense of what 'beyond' can mean.

To know me, close your eyes
and leave the road of affirmation,
the road of thinking and imagining:
just be a pilgrim to yourself,
alert, not knowing where to go,
but trusting in your ignorance
and travelling inward all the time.
Observe the spirals of your thoughts,
the interlace of hopes and fears
feeding off each other endlessly;
watch circles of your good intentions
revolving ineffectually,
the circles of jealousy and resentment –
just watch your convoluting self
proliferate without your intervening
until it dies away to nothing
but silence, a perfect stillness.
And if you bear the beautiful eeriness
of being aware without your I,
then home may come to you
as you surrender everything familiar,
a dispatching tenaciously resisted
because it feels like dying –
waiting for the other to come,
the initial lightening of atmosphere,
the shift, thoughts evaporating
as your sense of self is disabled,
the glow of uncentred awareness –
a crack
a flood of light engulfing
your being, infusing you with love –
if then you see me you've become
the unstained love you sought in me –
then who is who?
The eyes through which you see are mine.'

The furze begins to trill again.

My inky sketch of a doodle
seems more alive, just then,
than bifurcated *Kells*
exhibited like musty lungs
beneath glass – for glazed eyes
and exquisitely bated breath,
and reproduced promiscuously
to an attenuated death.
If art is able to transform us,
perhaps it's something we must *do*,
not receive; the process
is the crux – the flame, the flow
of images, words, ideas,
in which we lose our selves,
if only for a second or two,
when we become *lux fluens*,
embodying the life-stream
that issues from the source, the Fountain,
and which returns us home
to God, truth, the omega point.
It doesn't matter what we make –
an illumination, a doodled face,
a flower bed or mosaic –
it will confer a temporary grace
that's like an anamnesis
of life's peregrinal venture,
the oarless journey on the ocean,
when, if faithful to the Other,
we unselfconsciously create
the chart we trust will show the way
to the Island of the Saints,
discovering that the lines we draw
we're actually overlaying

on lines already waiting for us,
those of our personal fate –
that parallel and cross
the lines of other lives
and all of us converging on the One.
But this we'll only realise
at the end of life or beyond –
unless we glimpse it in a dream
or revelation – just as when
the tapestry we've only seen
from behind as dangling threads,
the messy details of our story,
is now revealed, and home at last,
we see our pattern in brocaded glory,
the confluence of lines of light.

3

Leaves

Leaves

Homer, Iliad VI, ll.146–50

Our lives are like the cycle of leaves.
The wind scatters the old leaves across the earth,
then spring returns and trees put forth new growth.
That's how it is with human beings:
the generations come and go, go and come.

The Summer World

from *In Loco Parentis*

for Rob

It irks me I don't remember much
about the days between the last exam
and the end. Did we party, or slouch
towards that unbearable freedom?
Weren't there rumours and plots?
Smuggling a sheep into Herbie's study,
streaking at supper, an alarm clock
primed to go off during Speech Day?
So I ring you, ahead of our weekly ritual,
tightening my grip on the receiver
until the click, sound of a shuffle,
TV blaring, whirr of your wheelchair.
We sound like beret-wearing veterans
forgetting we've spoken the week before,
eager to re-live anything we can.
I guide us, gently, to our final summer
and hear your brain working hard
as if you're in the middle of French Oral.
Eventually you say: 'I was feeling good.
The last exam – History? – went well.
It was a long hot summer, wasn't it?
I remember walking by Gatley's Pond
and stopping, feeling at ease… that's right –
I heard youngsters in the swimming pool.
It was so hot I'd taken off my shirt,
wearing just my corduroy waistcoat.
I can't remember where I'd come from…
or where I had to go…
just the heat, laughter and happy shouts…
And then there was the first eleven,

my final match – fifteen not out! –
the shock of mum arriving with a wig on.
Wigs were really awful at that time.
They never told me she was so ill;
they didn't want to ruin my exams.
She died the day before my results.
Three 'A's. That morning… I didn't know what…'
You stop-start to the end of the sentence,
but your words are merely sounds,
for I have drifted back to school,
the sunny path beside the pond,
and there you are, weightless, peaceful,
listening to the laughter of children,
happy and invisible.

His Father's Ghost

Virgil, Aeneid VI, ll. 684–702

Anchises saw Aeneas walk towards him
across the grass and held his hands out
and wept; words tumbled from his mouth:
'My son, my son! Are you really here at last?
I had such faith your sense of duty
would keep you going on that brutal voyage –
I feel so blessed to see your face again
and talk to you and hear your lovely voice.
For ages I've been fretting over when
you'd come – I knew you would. How right I was!
What distant lands and oceans did you cross
to get here? What dangers did you meet?
I worried that you'd come to harm in Libya.'
  Aeneas then replied: 'Your ghost, dear father –
I saw your poor sad ghost repeatedly
and it spurred me on to reach this twilight realm;
my ships are anchored on the Etruscan Sea.
Now, father, let me hold you – no *don't* withdraw!'
With these words, and with tears in his eyes,
he tried to hug his father's neck three times…
but three times the ghost slipped from his arms
as if it were a breeze or just a fleeting dream.

Portora Royal

from *In Loco Parentis*

We're like a troupe of travelling players,
the six of us rehearsing holiday roles
as we motor through the Irish midlands,
the sky blending with layers of turf smoke.
At Enniskillen we enter Dad's old school,
out-of-term deserted, a huge sepulchre,
headmaster with a warm off-duty smile,
showing us our rooms in the sanatorium;
then guiding us, like prospective parents,
to classrooms, dining hall; conjuring up
Beckett, vulpine in his cricket flannels,
and Oscar Wilde casting pearls to swine,
while Dad slips back some forty years –
me a mere three weeks – to homesickness.
Next day a change of emptiness: Lough Erne,
headmaster's boat, glare-induced smiles,
islands slipping past us on the water,
Dad acting the husband without a mistress,
Mum the unsuspecting wife.
Next day sickness strikes, a tummy bug,
and it's like a scene from *Endgame*,
all six of us in the sanatorium moaning
like mourners, and none of us knowing
that this will be our last family holiday,
but all of us knowing.

Prof

i.m. Professor Gordon Hamilton-Fairley (1930–1975)

At home that autumn morning
I heard the radio blur...
'a car bomb... no warning
Campden Hill Square
man dead... device set off
by his dog'... *please God
don't let it be the Prof.*

I used to wonder what
on earth he thought of me,
his daughter's boyfriend
arriving late, post-party,
toothbrush stuffed in denims,
squiffy, slurring words.
Yet he was always gracious
although he'd been on wards
all week, staring at death;
or conducting seminars
on lymphomas, leukaemia;
or lowering the blood pressure
of staff at St Bartholomew's.
I felt as if I'd lost a dad
again – the listener
I'd never really had;
a soulful empathiser.

I can see him at their cottage,
light fading as he pokes
a hedge to find a guinea pig
and save it from the fox;
nineteen-fifties retro

side-parted auburn hair,
an open face, crooked elbow,
attentive, ready to share
the countdown of his days;
for we had no idea
that he, a cancer specialist,
was fighting cancer too.

'Death of a Life Saver'
the headlines said. The bomb
was planted for a neighbour
delayed from leaving home.
Fate had dealt its cards,
was waiting: windows imploded
in the square; from body parts
they identified his elbow.
I went to Holland Park
and joined the family
delirious with shock
crying, laughing, alternately;
that night the four of them
slept together in one bed,
a tangled heap of limbs
like the raft of the *Medusa*.

The evening of the service
Mum and I met Dad
in his Fleet Street office,
the two of them re-glued
just for an hour or so;
it was like the old days –
them dressing up to go
to a West End premiere.
Dad asked about my tie
and looked a little miffed

when I replied
that it had been the Prof's.
We headed for St Paul's,
the sky gunpowder grey,
Dad musing on the war
when bombs were two a penny.
We thought a hundred souls
would come, but thousands
filled the floodlit cupola:
it was as if all London
was in mourning, the dome
rising like a huge balloon
on a myriad candle flames
and breath of hymns.
Afterwards we went back home:
Dad to his second wife
me to my single Mum;
the Prof's four children to a life
without their Dad.

In the cathedral crypt,
Dear Prof, your plaque
declares in stone that it
matters not how a man dies
but how he lives:
a bomb may vaporise us
but cannot even bruise
the memories of gestures,
and acts of mercy or malice
that stamp us thereafter.
Like placing a device
beneath a vehicle;
or saving a guinea pig
while Fate, like a fox,
is waiting in a field.

Carpe Diem

after Horace, Odes, *Book 1, 11*

for Adrian Frazier

We cannot know what Fate has planned for us,
so don't worry or bother reading tea leaves.
God knows, we could enjoy a few more winters –
or maybe this one, smashing huge waves
against the rocks, will be our last? Who's to say?
Be wise, relax, enjoy a good red wine
and trim your hopes to match a life that's brief.
Even as I write these words, begrudging time
is slipping by. So, come on, *seize the day*:
trusting the future's a recipe for grief.

Letter to Charles Harpur

i.m. Charles Harpur (1813–68)

for Kevin Brophy and Penelope Buckley

Dear Charles,
I never got as far as Singleton,
Jerry's Plains, or Eurobodalla,
your farm above the banked lane
of grassy verges and eucalyptus;
your grave, and that of Charles, your son
embedded by the farmhouse.
I *did* see Windsor, and tried in vain
to imagine you as a youngster
from your sepia daguerrotype –
like an old Confederate soldier,
waterfall beard, greyish white,
the baleful stare of Elijah.
Nearby, your friend, the Hawkesbury,
uncoiled through autumn fields;
and Homer was whispering in the trees –
my favourite lines were yours as well:
The race of men is as the race of leaves:
some the winds shed upon the ground, while still
the fructifying boughs put others forth,
to flourish in their season. So of men
the generations die and are renewed.

You wrote that after floods ruined
your farm, the first flush of TB,
and Charles's death had broken you.
Then came your self-obituary:

Here lies Charles Harpur,
who at fifty years of age
came to the conclusion,
that he was living in a sham age,
under a sham Government,
and amongst sham friends,
and that any World whatever
must therefore be
a better world than theirs...

I can hardly bear to think about
your purgatory before death,
the fading of your errant quest
to wrestle poetry from truth
in a brave new New South Wales
constructed by Old World gentry
and daily floggings; no wonder you'd sail
to the wine-dark plain of Troy
as you sorted letters in a post office
or spent those years farming sheep
to scrape the time to write, then face
ordeal by rejection slip.

What kept you going? Faith? Or fear
of meeting Milton in the afterlife?
Or the magical ingress of ideas
appearing like your ducks in flight
following the windings of the vale, and still
enlarging lengthwise, and in places too
oft breaking off into solitary dots.
Or were you rapt by your Muse's eyes –
two midnights of passionate thought –
igniting images in your mind,
such as your beach crab, who waits
for his prey amid the wave-washed stones

that glisten to the sun — gleaming himself
whenever he moves, as if his wetted shell
were breaking into flame.

Your parents brought you rootless
into a land of grog and marsupials.
Did you ever ask your father, Joseph,
about his childhood in Kinsale?
Or orientate yourself with stories
of family lore, like those I heard –
how, in the wake of Richard de Clare,
we Harpurs came to Wexford?
Or of your father's coffin-voyage
across the southern seas, to join
the tribe of Sisyphus and forge
the down-Underworld of Britain?

But you, convicted of your dream
to be the laureate of your nation,
transported yourself to a realm
beyond the Blue Mountains
and discovered... not 'China' –
the Shangri-La of convict fantasies –
but a dawn sky, *trees moist with dew*
and glinting all with a dim silveriness;
or *the sinuous valley of the waters;*
or *wide warm fields, glad with corn.*
You knew that nature had a sacred source
even as a sunbeam's fountain is the sun
and tried to open people's eyes.
But all they saw was a fool of God,
a voice de-crying in the wilderness,
soul-dwarfing priesthoods
and prone to drink, self-pity – yet seeing
deep down into the life of things:

and *what is deep is holy, and must tend*
to some divinely universal end.

Sham age, government, friends –
anywhere but Eurobodalla
seemed a blessing in the end.
I picture your deathbed tableau,
the spectral figure of Despair,
head bowed, pretending to grieve;
but Mary, too, sitting there
recalling your courtship; and shelves
of unread pages, hibernating
like winter trees, to open
somewhere in a future spring,
in leaf again.

Soracte

Horace, Odes, *Book 1, 9*

Just look at Mt Soracte aglitter
with snow, and those bending trees
slipping off their packs, and rivers
seized up, solid with thick ice.
Let's melt this cold. Heap logs on the fire!
Thaliarchus, pour the wine –
the vintage in the Sabine jar –
and don't dilute it, strong is fine;
the gods can deal with all the rest,
they who stop the hurricanes
lashing the sea, letting the cypress
and ancient ash fall still again.

Don't fret about tomorrow –
that Fortune brings it is a bonus;
you have an age before the woes
of decrepitude; enjoy your youth,
go dancing, have a love affair.
Now is the time for moonlit trysts,
for whispers in a city square
or in a field, perhaps a kiss;
the time for hidden giggling
from a girl in some nook or cove,
for snatching from her mock-resisting
finger, a token of her love.

Seraphim of Sarov

after a conversation between Nicholas Motovilov
and Seraphim in November 1831

The day was born in twilight,
grey above the forest glade,
the earth deepening with snow
as snow kept falling from the sky;
the fields pure white below the hill
beside the River Sarovka.
I sat on a stump opposite him;
all I could smell was fir trees.
'The only thing in life,' he said,
is to make ourselves a home
to welcome the holy spirit.
Nothing more. All else will follow.
Our souls use words for prayer,
but when the spirit descends
we must stay silent...'
I glanced at him: imagine
staring at the centre of the sun
and there you see someone's face,
lips moving, eyes expressive,
and you hear a voice speaking,
feel your shoulders being held
by hands you cannot see;
in fact you do not even see yourself,
just a dazzling light, diffusing
and making the glade luminous
and the snowflakes layering the snow.
I felt such peace in my soul;
no words could express it.
And such warmth.
No words can express it.

Acknowledgements

Some of these poems first appeared in the following publications: *Agenda, Atlanta Review, Bow-Wow Shop, Cork Literary Review, The Deep Heart's Core: Irish Poets Revisit a Touchstone* (Dedalus Press), *The Enchanting Verses* (India), *Watching My Hands at Work: A Festschrift for Adrian Frazier* (Salmon Poetry), *Hodges Figgis 250th anniversary anthology, Image, The Irish Times, Poem, Poetry International, Poetry Ireland Review, New Hibernian Review, New Humanist, Stinging Fly, Temenos Academy Review, Trinity Poets: An Anthology* (Carcanet Press).

'Kells' originated from a commission by the Poetry Society, for which many thanks to Christina Patterson. I was also greatly helped in writing the poem by a Patrick and Katherine Kavanagh Fellowship, a residency at the Princess Grace Irish Library, Monaco, and a Hawthornden Fellowship.

A number of poems have been broadcast on RTÉ's *Sunday Miscellany*. 'Prof' was broadcast on BBC Radio Four. Poems from *In Loco Parentis* are from a sequence that won the 2016 Vincent Buckley Poetry Prize.

A number of people have given me literary advice and encouragement during the making of this book. I would like to thank in particular Penelope Buckley, Hilary Davies, John F. Deane, Alyson Hallett and Grace Wells.

Special thanks to Ian Wild, for all his wisdom, literary and otherwise; to Francesca Diano for her translations; Patrick Cotter of the Munster Literature Centre for his continued support; Kevin Brophy for his kindness in Australia; Ian McDonagh and Cork County Arts and the Arts Council of Ireland / An Chomhairle Ealaíon, for invaluable literary bursaries; Michael, Luke and Katie at Carcanet for their midwifery; and Rosemary, Sarah, Merrily, Pat, Evie and Gracie.